MW00934745

This Notebook belongs to:

Made in the USA
Las Vegas, NV
28 August 2021

29157996R00083